FOR

FROM

DATE

HELEN STEINER RICE

A COLLECTION OF
Hope

Teal Press

Published in the UK by Teal Press Ltd.

ISBN: 978-0-99560-252-6

This English-language edition issued by special arrangement with:
Barbour Publishing, Inc.,
P.O. Box 719
Uhrichsville, Ohio, U.S.A.

A CIP catalogue record for this book is available from the British Library.

Acknowledgements:

Scripture verses marked (NIV) taken from the Holy Bible,
New International Version®.
NIV® Copyright ©1973, 1978, 1984, 2011 by Biblica, Inc.®
Used by permission. All rights reserved worldwide.

Scripture verses marked (NKJV) taken from the Holy Bible,
New King James Version®.
Copyright © 1982 by Thomas Nelson.
Used by permission. All rights reserved.

Scripture verses marked (NLT) taken from the Holy Bible,
New Living Translation.
Copyright © 1996, 2004, 2015 by Tyndale House Foundation.
Used by permission of Tyndale House Publishers Inc.,
Carol Stream, Illinois 60188. All rights reserved.

Cover Photo by Anna Antonova. Used under license from Shutterstock.com.

Contents

∽

∽

Peaceful Reflections

Peace I leave with you; my peace I give you. I do not give to you as the world gives. Do not let your hearts be troubled and do not be afraid.

John 14:27 (NIV)

Helen Steiner Rice

After Each Storm of Life, There's a Rainbow Hope

The rainbow is God's promise
of hope for you and me,
And though the clouds hang
heavy and the sun we cannot see,
We know above the dark
clouds that fill the stormy sky,
Hope's rainbow will come shining through
when the clouds have drifted by.

A Beautiful Beginning
for Peace on Earth

Let us all remember when
our faith is running low,
Christ is more than just a figure
wrapped in an ethereal glow ...
For He came and dwelled among
us and He knows our every need,
And He loves and understands
us and forgives each sinful deed.
He was crucified and buried
and rose again in glory,
And His promise of salvation
makes the wondrous Christmas story
An abiding reassurance that
the little Christ child's birth
Was the beautiful beginning of
God's plan for peace on earth.

Helen Steiner Rice

No Favor Do I Seek Today

I come not to ask, to plead, or implore -
I just come to tell You how much I adore You.
For to kneel in Your presence makes me feel blessed,
For I know that You know all my needs best,
And it fills me with joy just to linger with you,
As my soul You replenish and my heart You renew.
For prayer is much more than just asking for things -
It's the peace and contentment that quietness brings.
So thank You again for Your mercy and love
And for making me heir to Your kingdom above.

It's a Wonderful World

In spite of the fact we complain and lament
And view this old world with much discontent,
Deploring conditions and grumbling because
There's so much injustice and so many flaws,
It's a wonderful world and it always will be
If we keep our eyes open and focused to see
The wonderful things we are capable of
When we open our hearts to God and His love.

Helen Steiner Rice

The Happiness You Already Have

Memories are treasures that
time cannot destroy,
They are the happy pathway
to yesterday's bright joy.

☙

Life

☙

A little laughter, a little song,
A little teardrop
When things go wrong,
A little calm
And a little strife
A little loving
And that is life.

☙

Peace Begins in the Home and the Heart

Peace is not something you fight
for with bombs and missiles that kill.
Peace is attained in the silence that
comes when the heart stands still.
For hearts that are restless and
warlike with longings that never cease
Can never contribute ideas that
bring the world nearer to peace.
For as dew never falls on a morning
that follows a dark, stormy night,
The peace and grace of our Father
fall not on a soul in flight.
So if we seek peace for all people,
there is but one place to begin,
And the armament race will not win it,
for the fortress of peace is within.

❧

Helen Steiner Rice

The Masterpiece

Framed by the vast, unlimited sky,
Bordered by mighty waters,
Sheltered by beautiful woodland groves,
Scented with flowers that bloom and die,
Protected by giant mountain peaks -
The land of the great unknown -
Snowcapped and towering, a nameless place
That beckons man on as the gold he seeks,
Bubbling with life and earthly joys,
Reeking with pain and mortal strife,
Dotted with wealth and material gains,
Built on ideals of girls and boys,
Streaked with toil, opportunity's banner unfurled
Stands out the masterpiece of art
Painted by the one great God,
A picture of the world.

The Comfort and Sweetness of Peace

After the clouds, the sunshine,
After the winter, the spring,
After the shower, the rainbow -
For life is a changeable thing.
After the night, the morning,
Bidding all darkness cease,
After life's cares and sorrows,
The comfort and sweetness of peace.

Helen Steiner Rice

A Word of Understanding

May peace and understanding
Give you strength and courage, too,
And may the hours and days ahead
Hold a new hope for you;
For the sorrow that is yours today
Will pass away; and then
You'll find the sun of happiness
Will shine for you again.

The Comfort of Friends

The heartfelt counsel of a friend
is as sweet as perfume and incense.
Proverbs 27:9 (NLT)

Helen Steiner Rice

Discouragement and Dreams

So many things in the line of duty
Drain us of effort and leave us no beauty,
And the dust of the soul grows thick and unswept,
The spirit is drenched in tears unwept.
But just as we fall beside the road,
Discouraged with life and
bowed down with our load,
We lift our eyes, and what seemed a dead end
Is the street of dreams where we meet a friend.

Friends Are Life's Gift of Love

If people like me didn't know people like you,
Life would lose its meaning and its richness, too.
For the friends that we make are life's gift of love,
And I think friends are sent right from heaven above.
And thinking of you somehow makes me feel
That God is love and He's very real.

~

Helen Steiner Rice

The Gift of Friendship

Friendship is a priceless gift
that cannot be bought or sold,
But its value is far greater than
a mountain made of gold -
For gold is cold and lifeless,
it can neither see nor hear,
And in the time of trouble it
is powerless to cheer.
It has no ears to listen,
no heart to understand,
It cannot bring you comfort or
reach out a helping hand -
So when you ask God for a gift
be thankful if He sends
Not diamonds, pearls, or riches,
but the love of real true friends.

The Joy of Unselfish Giving

Time is not measured by the years that you live
But by the deeds that you do and
the joy that you give.
And from birthday to birthday,
the good Lord above
Bestows on His children the gift of His love,
Asking us only to share it with others
By treating all people not as strangers
but brothers.
And each day as it comes brings
a chance to each one
To live to the fullest, leaving nothing undone
That would brighten the life or lighten the load
Of some weary traveler lost on life's road.
So it doesn't matter how long we may live
If as long as we live we unselfishly give.

Helen Steiner Rice

Life Is a Garden

Life is a garden; good friends are the flowers,
And times spent together life's happiest hours.
And friendship, like flowers, blooms ever more fair
When carefully tended by dear friends who care.
And life's lovely garden would be sweeter by far
If all who passed through it were as nice as you are.

Strangers Are Friends We Haven't Met Yet

God knows no strangers, He loves us all,
The poor, the rich, the great, the small.
He is a friend who is always there
To share our troubles and lessen our care.
For no one is a stranger in God's sight,
For God is love, and in His light
May we, too, try in our small way
To make new friends from day to day.
So pass no stranger with an unseeing eye,
For God may be sending a new friend by.

Helen Steiner Rice

The Garden of Friendship

There is no garden
So complete
But roses could make
The place more sweet.
There is no life
So rich and rare
But one more friend
Could enter there.
Like roses in a garden
Kindness fills the air
With a certain bit of sweetness
As it touches everywhere.

My God Is No Stranger

God is no stranger in a faraway place
He's as close as the wind that blows 'cross my face.
It's true I can't see the wind as it blows,
But I feel it around me and my heart surely knows
That God's mighty hand can be felt everywhere,
For there's nothing on earth that is not in God's care.
The sky and the stars, the waves and the sea,
The dew on the grass, the leaves on a tree
Are constant reminders of God and His nearness
Proclaiming His presence with crystal-like clearness.
So how could I think God was far, far away
When I feel Him beside me every hour of the day?
And I've plenty of reasons to know God's my friend,
And this is one friendship that time cannot end.

Helen Steiner Rice

Joy in All Circumstances

May the God of hope fill you with all joy and peace
as you trust in him, so that you may overflow
with hope by the power of the Holy Spirit.

Romans 15:13 (NIV)

Helen Steiner Rice

How Great the Yield
from a Fertile Field

The farmer plows through the fields of green,
And the blade of the plow is sharp and keen,
But the seed must be sown to bring forth grain,
For nothing is born without suffering and pain,
And God never plows in the soul of man
Without intention and purpose and plan ...
So whenever you feel the plow's sharp blade
Let not your heart be sorely afraid,
For like the farmer, God chooses a field
From which He expects an excellent yield ...
So rejoice though your heart be broken in two -
God seeks to bring forth a rich harvest in you.

Meet Life's Trials with Smiles

There are times when life overwhelms
us and our trials seem too many to bear,
It is then we should stop to remember
God is standing by ready to share
The uncertain hours that confront
us and fill us with fear and despair,
For God in His goodness has promised
that the cross that He gives us to wear
Will never exceed our endurance or
be more than our strength can bear ...
And secure in that blessed assurance,
we can smile as we face tomorrow,
For God holds the key to the future,
and no sorrow or care we need borrow.

Helen Steiner Rice

Expectation! Anticipation! Realization!

God gives us a power we so seldom employ,
For we're so unaware it is filled with such joy.
The gift that God gives us is anticipation,
Which we can fulfill with sincere expectation,
For there's power in belief when
we think we will find
Joy for the heart and peace for the mind,
And believing the day will bring a surprise
Is not only pleasant but surprisingly wise.
For we open the door to let joy walk through
When we learn to expect the best,
and the most, too,
And believing we'll find a happy surprise
Makes reality out of a fancied surmise.

Giving Is the Key to Living

Every day is a reason for giving
And giving is the key to living.
So let us give ourselves away,
Not just today but every day,
And remember, a kind and thoughtful deed
Or a hand outstretched in a time of need
Is the rarest of gifts, for it is a part,
Not of the purse but a loving heart.
And he who gives of himself will find
True joy of heart and peace of mind.

Helen Steiner Rice

Lives Distressed Cannot Be Blessed

Refuse to be discouraged, refuse to be distressed,
For when we are despondent,
our lives cannot be blessed,
For doubt and fear and worry close
the door to faith and prayer,
And there's no room for blessings
when we're lost in deep despair.
So remember when you're troubled
with uncertainty and doubt,
It is best to tell our Father what
our fear is all about,
For unless we seek His guidance
when troubled times arise,
We are bound to make decisions
that are twisted and unwise,
But when we view our problems
through the eyes of God above,
Misfortunes turn to blessings and
hatred turns to love.

A Sure Way to a Happy Day

Happiness is something we create in our minds;
It's not something you search for and so seldom find.
It's just waking up and beginning the day
By counting our blessings and kneeling to pray.
It's giving up thoughts that breed discontent
And accepting what comes as a gift heaven-sent.
It's giving up wishing for things we have not
And making the best of whatever we've got.
It's knowing that life is determined for us
And pursuing our tasks without fret, fume, or fuss.
For it's by completing what God gives us to do
That we find real contentment and happiness, too.

∽

Helen Steiner Rice

Be Glad

Be glad that your life has been full and complete,
Be glad that you've tasted the bitter and sweet.
Be glad that you've walked in sunshine and rain,
Be glad that you've felt both pleasure and pain.
Be glad that you've had such a full, happy life,
Be glad for your joy as well as your strife.
Be glad that you've walked with courage each day,
Be glad you've had strength for each step of the way.
Be glad for the comfort that you've found in prayer.
Be glad for God's blessings, His love, and His care.

Abundant Thanksgiving

Giving thanks always for all things unto God and the
Father in the name of our Lord Jesus Christ.

Ephesians 5:20

Helen Steiner Rice

A Thankful Heart

Take nothing for granted, for whenever you do,
The joy of enjoying is lessened for you.
For we rob our own lives much
more than we know
When we fail to respond or in any way show
Our thanks for the blessings that daily are ours -
The warmth of the sun, the fragrance of flowers,
The beauty of twilight, the freshness of dawn,
The coolness of dew on a green velvet lawn,
The kind little deeds so thoughtfully done,
The favors of friends and the love that someone
Unselfishly gives us in a myriad of ways,
Expecting no payment and no words of praise.
Oh, great is our loss when we no longer find
A thankful response to things of this kind.
For the joy of enjoying and the fullness of living
Are found in the heart that is
filled with thanksgiving.

A Heart Full of Thanksgiving

Everyone needs someone to be thankful for,
And each day of life we are aware of this more,
For the joy of enjoying and the fullness of living
Are found only in hearts that are filled
with thanksgiving.

৩

A Prayer of Thanks

৩

Thank You, God, for the
beauty around me everywhere,
The gentle rain and glistening dew,
the sunshine and the air,
The joyous gift of feeling the soul's soft,
whispering voice
That speaks to me from deep within
and makes my heart rejoice.

৩

Helen Steiner Rice

Showers of Blessings

Each day there are showers of
blessings sent from the Father above,
For God is a great, lavish giver,
and there is no end to His love.
And His grace is more than sufficient,
His mercy is boundless and deep,
And His infinite blessings are countless,
and all this we're given to keep
If we but seek God and find Him
and ask for a bounteous measure
Of this wholly immeasurable offering
from God's inexhaustible treasure.
For no matter how big man's dreams are,
God's blessings are infinitely more,
For always God's giving is greater
than what man is asking for.

If You Meet God in the Morning

Each day at dawning I lift my heart high
And raise up my eyes to the infinite sky.
I watch the night vanish as a new day is born,
And I hear the birds sing on the wings of the morn.
I see the dew glisten in crystal-like splendor
While God, with a touch that is gentle and tender,
Wraps up the night and softly tucks it away
And hangs out the sun to herald a new day.
And so I give thanks and my heart kneels to pray,
"God, keep me and guide me and go with me today."

Helen Steiner Rice

Things to Be Thankful For

The good, green earth beneath our feet,
The air we breathe, the food we eat,
Some work to do, a goal to win,
A hidden longing deep within
That spurs us on to bigger things
And helps us meet what each day brings -
All these things and many more
Are things we should be thankful for ...
And most of all, our thankful prayers
Should rise to God because He cares.

c⁓

Unfailing Love

For God so loved the world
that He gave His only begotten Son,
that whoever believes in Him should not perish
but have everlasting life.

John 3:16 (NKJV)

Helen Steiner Rice

He Loves You

ⵦ

It's amazing and incredible,
but it's as true as it can be -
God loves and understands us all,
and that means you and me.
His grace is all-sufficient for
both the young and old,
For the lonely and the timid,
for the brash and for the bold.
His love knows no exceptions,
so never feel excluded,
No matter who or what you are,
your name has been included ...
And no matter what your past has been,
trust God to understand,
And no matter what your problem is,
just place it in His hand ...
For in all our unloveliness this
great God loves us still -
He loved us since the world began,
and what's more, He always will!

ⵦ

Stepping Stones to God

An aching heart is but a stepping stone
To greater joy than you've ever known,
For things that cause the heart to ache
Until you think that it must break
Become the strength by which we climb
To higher heights that are sublime
And feel the radiance of God's smiles
When we have soared above life's trials.
So when you're overwhelmed with fears
And all your hopes are drenched in tears,
Think not that life has been unfair
And given you too much to bear,
For God has chosen you because,
With all your weaknesses and flaws,
He feels that you are worthy of
The greatness of his wondrous love.

Helen Steiner Rice

Never Be Discouraged

∽

There is really nothing we need
know or even try to understand
If we refuse to be discouraged
and trust God's guiding hand,
So take heart and meet each minute
with faith in God's great love,
Aware that every day of life is
controlled by God above
And never dread tomorrow
or what the future brings
Just pray for strength and courage
and trust God in all things,
And never grow discouraged -
be patient and just wait,
For God never comes too early,
and He never comes too late.

∽

The Magic of Love

Love is like magic and it always will be,
For love still remains life's sweet mystery.
Love works in ways that are
wondrous and strange,
And there's nothing in life that
love cannot change.
Love can transform the most commonplace
Into beauty and splendor and
sweetness and grace.
Love is unselfish, understanding, and kind,
For it sees with its heart and not with its mind.
Love gives and forgives; there is nothing too much
For love to heal with its magic touch.
Love is the language that every heart speaks,
For love is the one thing that every heart seeks ...
And where there is love God, too, will abide
And bless the family residing inside.

Helen Steiner Rice

Wings of Love

The priceless gift of life is love,
For with the help of God above
Love can change the human race
And make this world a better place ...
For love dissolves all hate and fear
And makes our vision bright and clear
So we can see and rise above
Our pettiness on wings of love.

Do Not Be Anxious

Do not be anxious, said our Lord,
Have peace from day to day -
The lilies neither toil nor spin,
Yet none are clothed as they.
The meadowlark with sweetest song
Fears not for bread or nest
Because he trusts our Father's love,
And God knows what is best.

Helen Steiner Rice

God Is Never Beyond Our Reach

No one ever sought the Father
and found He was not there,
And no burden is too heavy
to be lightened by a prayer.
No problem is too intricate,
and no sorrow that we face
Is too deep and devastating
to be softened by His grace.
No trials and tribulations are
beyond what we can bear
If we share them with our Father
as we talk to Him in prayer ...

God Loves Us

We are all God's children
and He loves us, every one.
He freely and completely
forgives all that we have done,
Asking only if we're ready to
follow where He leads,
Content that in His wisdom
He will answer all our needs.

Helen Steiner Rice

The Hand of God Is Everywhere

It's true we have never looked on His face,
But His likeness shines forth from every place,
For the hand of God is everywhere
Along life's busy thoroughfare,
And His presence can be felt and seen
Right in the midst of our daily routine.
Things we touch and see and feel
Are what make God so very real.

Seasons of Hope

He shall be like a tree
Planted by the rivers of water,
That brings forth its fruit in its season,
Whose leaf also shall not wither;
And whatever he does shall prosper.
Psalm 1:3 (NKJV)

Helen Steiner Rice

The Blessings of God's Seasons

We know we must pass through
the seasons God sends,
Content in the knowledge that everything ends,
And oh, what a blessing to know there are reasons
And to find that our souls must,
too, have their seasons -
Bounteous seasons and barren ones, too,
Times for rejoicing and times to be blue -
But meeting these seasons of dark desolation
With the strength that is born of anticipation
Comes from knowing that every season of sadness
Will surely be followed by a springtime of gladness.

Slowing Down

My days are so crowded and my hours so few
And I can no longer work fast like I used to do.
But I know I must learn to be satisfied,
That God has not completely denied
The joy of working - at a much slower pace -
For as long as He gives me a little place
To work with Him in His vineyard of love,
Just to know that He's helping me from above
Gives me strength to meet each day
As I travel along life's changing way.

Helen Steiner Rice

Spring Awakens What Autumn Puts to Sleep

A garden of asters in varying hues,
Crimson pinks and violet blues,
Blossoming in the hazy fall,
Wrapped in autumn's lazy pall ...
But early frost stole in one night,
And like a chilling, killing blight
It touched each pretty aster's head,
And now the garden's still and dead,
And all the lovely flowers that bloomed
Will soon be buried and entombed
In winter's icy shroud of snow ...
But oh, how wonderful to know
That after winter comes the spring
To breathe new life in everything,
And all the flowers that fell in death
Will be awakened by spring's breath ...
For in God's plan both men and flowers
Can only reach bright, shining hours
By dying first to rise in glory
And prove again the Easter story.

I Come to Meet You

I come to meet You, God, and as I linger here
I seem to feel You very near.
A rustling leaf, a rolling slope
Speak to my heart of endless hope.
The sun just rising in the sky,
The waking birdlings as they fly,
The grass all wet with morning dew
Are telling me I just met You ...
And gently thus the day is born
As night gives way to breaking morn,
And once again I've met You, God,
And worshipped on Your holy sod ...
For who could see the dawn break through
Without a glimpse of heaven and You?
For who but God could make the day
And softly put the night away?

Helen Steiner Rice

All Nature Proclaims
Eternal Life

Flowers sleeping 'neath the snow,
Awakening when the spring winds blow,
Leafless trees so bare before
Gowned in lacy green once more,
Hard, unyielding, frozen sod
Now softly carpeted by God,
Still streams melting in the spring
Rippling over rocks that sing,
Barren, windswept, lonely hills
Turning gold with daffodils -
These miracles are all around
Within our sight and touch and sound,
As true and wonderful today
As when the stone was rolled away,
Proclaiming to all doubting men
That in God all things live again.

⌒

Growing Older Is Part of God's Plan

You can't hold back the dawn
or stop the tides from flowing
Or keep a rose from withering
or still a wind that's blowing,
And time cannot be halted in
its swift and endless flight,
For age is sure to follow youth
like day comes after night ...
For He who sets our span of
years and watches from above
Replaces youth and beauty
with peace and truth and love,
And then our souls are privileged
to see a hidden treasure
That in youth escapes our eyes
in our pursuit of pleasure ...
So passing years are but blessings
that open up the way
To the everlasting beauty
of God's eternal day.

Helen Steiner Rice

Life's Golden Autumn

∽

Memory opens wide the door
on a happy day like this,
And with a sweet nostalgia
we longingly recall,
The happy days of long ago
that seem the best of all ...
But time cannot be halted in
its swift and endless flight,
And age is sure to follow youth
as day comes after night,
And once again it's proven that
the restless brain of man
Is powerless to alter God's great,
unchanging plan ...
But while our steps grow slower
and we grow more tired, too,
The soul goes roaring upward
to realms untouched and new,
Where God's children live forever
in the beauty of His love.

∽

Each Spring God Renews His Promise

Long, long ago in a land far away,
There came the dawn of the first Easter day,
And each year we see the promise reborn
That God gave the world on that first Easter morn.
For in each waking flower and each singing bird
The promise of Easter is witnessed and heard,
And spring is God's way of speaking to men
And renewing the promise of Easter again ...
For death is a season that man must pass through,
And just like the flowers, God wakens him, too,
So why should we grieve when our loved ones die,
For we'll meet them again in a cloudless sky.
For Easter is more than a beautiful story -
It's the promise of life and eternal glory.

Helen Steiner Rice

God's Unfailing Birthday Promise

From one birthday to another
God will gladly give
To everyone who seeks Him and
tries each day to live
A little bit more closely to
God and to each other,
Seeing everyone who passes as a
neighbor, friend, or brother,
Not only joy and happiness but
the faith to meet each trial
Not with fear and trepidation
but with an inner smile ...
For we know life's never measured
by how many years we live
But by the kindly things we do
and the happiness we give.

ↄ

The Autumn of Life

∽

What a wonderful time is life's autumn,
when the leaves of the trees are all gold,
When God fills each day as He sends
it with memories, priceless and old.
What a treasure-house filled with rare
jewels are the blessings of year upon year,
When life has been lived as you've lived it
in a home where God's presence is near ...
May the deep meaning surrounding this day,
like the paintbrush of God up above,
Touch your life with wonderful blessings.

∽

Helen Steiner Rice

This Is Just a Resting Place

Sometimes the road of life seems
long as we travel through the years
And with a heart that's broken
and eyes brimful of tears,
We falter in our weariness
and sink beside the way,
But God leans down and whispers,
"Child, there'll be another day,"
And the road will grow much
smoother and much easier to face,
So do not be disheartened,
this is just a resting place.

The Power of Prayer

And I say unto you,
Ask, and it shall be given you; seek, and ye shall find;
knock, and it shall be opened unto you.

Luke 11:9

Helen Steiner Rice

The Heavenly Staircase

Prayers are the stairs that lead to God,
and there's joy every step of the way
When we make our pilgrimage to
Him with love in our hearts each day.

Power of Prayer

I am only a worker employed by the Lord,
And great is my gladness and rich my reward
If I can just spread the wonderful story
That God is the answer to eternal glory ...
Bringing new hope and comfort and cheer
Telling sad hearts there is nothing to fear,
And what greater joy could there be than to share
The love of God and the power of prayer?

On the Wings
of Prayer

On the wings of prayer our burdens take flight
And our load of care becomes bearably light
And our heavy hearts are lifted above
To be healed by the balm of God's wonderful love ...
And the tears in our eyes are dried by the hands
Of a loving Father who understands
All of our problems, our fears and despair
When we take them to Him on the
wings of prayer.

Helen Steiner Rice

The House of Prayer

Just close your eyes and open your heart
And feel your cares and worries depart.
Just yield yourself to the Father above
And let Him hold you secure in His love ...
For life on earth grows more involved
With endless problems that can't be solved,
But God only asks us to do our best,
Then He will take over and finish the rest ...
So when you are tired, discouraged, and blue,
There's always one door that is opened to you
And that is the door to the house of prayer,
And you'll find God waiting to meet you there ...
And the house of prayer is no farther away
Than the quiet spot where you kneel and pray.
For the heart is a temple when God is there
As we place ourselves in His loving care ...
And He hears every prayer and answers each one
When we pray in His name, "Thy will be done."
And the burdens that seemed too heavy to bear
Are lifted away on the wings of prayer.

God's Stairway

Step by step we climb day by day
Closer to God with each prayer we pray,
For the cry of the heart offered in prayer
Becomes just another spiritual stair
In the heavenly place where we live anew ...
So never give up, for it's worth the climb
To live forever in endless time
Where the soul of man is safe and free
To live and love through eternity.

Helen Steiner Rice

Show Me More Clearly the Way to Serve and Love You More Each Day

God, help me in my feeble way
To somehow do something each day
To show You that I love You best
And that my faith will stand each test,
And let me serve You every day
And feel You near me when I pray.
Oh, hear my prayer, dear God above,
And make me worthy of Your love.

A Part of Me

Dear God, You are a part of me -
You're all I do and all I see,
You're what I say and what I do,
For all my life belongs to You.
You walk with me and talk with me,
For I am Yours eternally,
And when I stumble, slip, and fall
Because I'm weak and lost and small,
You help me up and take my hand
And lead me toward the Promised Land.
I cannot dwell apart from You -
You would not ask or want me to,
For You have room within Your heart
To make each child of Yours a part
Of You and all Your love and care
If we but come to You in prayer.

Helen Steiner Rice

Talk It Over with God

You're worried and troubled about everything,
Wondering and fearing what tomorrow will bring.
You long to tell someone, for you feel so alone,
But your friends are all burdened
with cares of their own.
There is only one place and only one friend
Who is never too busy, and you can always depend
On Him to be waiting, with arms open wide
To hear all the troubles you came to confide ...
For the heavenly Father will always be there
When you seek Him and find Him at the
altar of prayer.

Abiding Faith

If you abide in Me, and My words abide in you,
you will ask what you desire, and it shall
be done for you.
John 15:7 (NKJV)

Helen Steiner Rice

Faith and Trust

Sometimes when a light
Goes out of our lives
And we are left in darkness
And we do not know which way to go,
We must put our hand
Into the hand of God
And ask Him to lead us
And if we let our lives become a prayer
Until we are strong enough
To stand under the weight
Of our own thoughts again,
Somehow, even the most difficult
Hours are bearable.

The Bend in the Road

Sometimes we come to life's crossroads
and view what we think is the end,
But God has a much wider vision,
and He knows it's only a bend.
The road will go on and get smoother,
and after we've stopped for a rest,
The path that lies hidden beyond
us is often the part that is best.
So rest and relax and grow stronger,
let go and let God share your load,
And have faith in a brighter tomorrow;
you've just come to a bend in the road.

Helen Steiner Rice

Now I Lay Me Down to Sleep

I remember so well this prayer I said
Each night as my mother tucked me in bed,
And today this same prayer is still the best way
To sign off with God at the end of the day
And to ask Him your soul to safely keep
As you wearily close your tired eyes in sleep,
Feeling content that the Father above
Will hold you secure in His great arms of love ...
And having His promise that if ere you wake
His angels reach down, your sweet soul to take
Is perfect assurance that, awake or asleep,
God is always right there to tenderly keep
All of His children ever safe in His care,
For God's here and He's there
and He's everywhere ...
So into His hands each night as I sleep
I commend my soul for the dear Lord to keep,
Knowing that if my soul should take flight
It will soar to the land where there is no night.

Yesterday, Today, and Tomorrow

Yesterday's dead, tomorrow's unborn,
So there's nothing to fear and nothing to mourn,
For all that is past and all that has been
Can never return to be lived once again ...
And what lies ahead or the things that will be
Are still in God's hands, so it is not up to me
To live in the future that is God's great unknown,
For the past and the present
God claims for His own ...
So all I need do is to live for today
And trust God to show me the truth and the way,
For it's only the memory of things that have been
And expecting tomorrow to bring trouble again
That fills my today, which God wants to bless,
With uncertain fears and borrowed distress ...
For all I need live for is this one little minute,
For life's here and now and eternity's in it.

Helen Steiner Rice

Somebody Loves You

Somebody loves you more than you know,
Somebody goes with you wherever you go,
Somebody really and truly cares
And lovingly listens to all of your prayers ...
Don't doubt for a minute that this is not true,
For God loves His children and
takes care of them, too ...
And all of His treasures are yours to share
If you love Him completely and
show that you care ...
And if you walk in His footsteps
and have faith to believe,
There's nothing you ask for that
you will not receive!

The Revelations of Easter

～

The waking earth in springtime
Reminds us it is true
That nothing ever really dies
That is not born anew ...
So trust God's all-wise wisdom
And doubt the Father never,
For in His heavenly kingdom
There is nothing lost forever.

～

Helen Steiner Rice

Fortress of Faith

It's easy to say "In God we trust"
when life is radiant and fair,
But the test of faith is only found
when there are burdens to bear.
For our claim to faith in the
sunshine is really no faith at all,
For when roads are smooth and days
are bright our need for God is so small.
And no one discovers the fullness
or the greatness of God's love
Unless they have walked in the
darkness with only a light from above.
For the faith to endure whatever comes
is born of sorrow and trials
And strengthened only by discipline
and nurtured by self-denials.
So be not disheartened by troubles,
for trials are the building blocks
On which to erect a fortress of faith,
secure on God's ageless rocks.

Faith Is a Candle

೦๑

In this sick world of hatred and violence and sin,
Where society renounces morals
and rejects discipline,
We stumble in darkness groping vainly for light
To distinguish the difference between
wrong and right.
But dawn cannot follow this night of despair
Unless faith lights a candle in
all hearts everywhere.
And warmed by the glow, our hate melts away
And love lights the path to a peaceful new day.

೦๑

Helen Steiner Rice

He Asks so Little and Gives so Much

What must I do to ensure peace of mind?
Is the answer I'm seeking too hard to find?
How can I know what God wants me to be?
How can I tell what's expected of me?
Where can I go for guidance and aid
To help me correct the errors I've made?
The answer is found in doing three things,
And great is the gladness that doing them brings.
"Do justice" - "Love kindness" -
"Walk humbly with God" -
For with these three things as
your rule and your rod,
All things worth having are yours to achieve,
If you follow God's words and have
faith to believe.

✁

We Can't, but God Can

Why things happen as they do
we do not always know,
And we cannot always fathom
why our spirits sink so low.
But all that is required of us
whenever things go wrong
Is to trust in God implicitly with
a faith that's deep and strong.
And while He may not instantly
unravel all the strands
Of the tangled thoughts that trouble us,
He completely understands -
And in His time, if we have faith,
He will gradually restore
The brightness to our spirits
that we've been longing for.
So remember there's no cloud too
dark for God's light to penetrate
If we keep on believing and have
faith enough to wait.

Helen Steiner Rice

Faith Is a Mover
of Mountains

Faith is a force that is greater
than knowledge or power or skill,
And the darkest defeat turns to triumph
if you trust in God's wisdom and will,
For faith is a mover of mountains -
there's nothing man cannot achieve
If he has the courage to try it
and then has the faith to believe.

Eternal Blessings

You have endowed him with eternal blessings
and given him the joy of your presence.

Psalm 21:6 (NLT)

Helen Steiner Rice

God's Jewels for You

We watch the rich and famous
bedecked in precious jewels,
Enjoying earthly pleasures, defying moral rules,
And in our mood of discontent
we sink into despair
And long for earthly riches and
feel cheated of our share ...
But stop these idle musings,
God has stored up for you
Treasures that are far beyond
earth's jewels and riches, too,
For never, never discount
what God has promised man
If he will walk in meekness
and accept God's flawless plan,
For if we heed His teaching as
we journey through the years,
We'll find the richest jewels of
all are crystallized from tears.

There Are Blessings in Everything

Blessings come in many guises
That God alone in love devises,
And sickness, which we dread so much,
Can bring a very healing touch,
For often on the wings of pain
The peace we sought before in vain
Will come to us with sweet surprise,
For God is merciful and wise ...
And through long hours of tribulation
God gives us time for meditation,
And no sickness can be counted loss
That teaches us to bear our cross.

Helen Steiner Rice

The Blessings of Sharing

Only what we give away
Enriches us from day to day,
For not in getting but in giving
Is found the lasting joy of living,
For no one ever had a part
In sharing treasures of the heart
Who did not feel the impact of
The magic mystery of God's love.
Love alone can make us kind
And give us joy and peace of mind,
So live with joy unselfishly,
And you'll be blessed abundantly.

What Is a Baby?

A baby is a gift of life born
of the wonder of love -
A little bit of eternity sent from the Father above,
Giving a new dimension to the love
between husband and wife
And putting an added new meaning
to the wonder and mystery of life.

God's Keeping

To be in God's keeping is surely a blessing,
For though life is often dark and distressing,
No day is too dark and no burden too great
That God in His love cannot penetrate.

Helen Steiner Rice

Motherhood

The dearest gifts that heaven holds,
the very finest, too,
Were made into one pattern that
was perfect, sweet, and true.
The angels smiled, well pleased, and said,
"Compared to all the others,
This pattern is so wonderful let's
use it just for mothers!"
And through the years, a mother has
been all that's sweet and good,
For there's a bit of God and love
in all true motherhood.

The Golden Years of Life

God in His loving and all-wise way
Makes the heart that once was too young yesterday
Serene and more gentle and less restless, too,
Content to remember the joys it once knew.
And all that we sought on the pathway of pleasure
Becomes but a memory to cherish and treasure -
The fast pace grows slower and the spirit serene,
And the soul can envision what
the eyes have not seen.
And so while life's springtime is sweet to recall,
The autumn of life is the best time of all,
For our wild youthful yearnings all gradually cease,
And God fills our days with beauty and peace!

c∽

Helen Steiner Rice

This Is My Father's World

Everywhere across the land
You see God's face and touch His hand
Each time you look up in the sky
Or watch the fluffy clouds drift by,
Or feel the sunshine, warm and bright,
Or watch the dark night turn to light,
Or hear a bluebird brightly sing,
Or see the winter turn to spring,
Or stop to pick a daffodil,
Or gather violets on some hill,
Or touch a leaf or see a tree,
It's all God whispering, "This is Me.
And I am faith and I am light,
And in Me there shall be no night."

Triumph Over Trials

For I, the Lord your God, will hold your right hand,

Saying to you, 'Fear not, I will help you.'

Isaiah 41:13 (NKJV)

Helen Steiner Rice

Traveling to Heaven

Life is a highway on which the years go by,
Sometimes the road is level,
sometimes the hills are high.
But as we travel onward to
a future that's unknown,
We can make each mile we travel
a heavenly stepping stone!

Burdens Can Be Blessings

Our Father knows what's best for us,
So why should we complain -
We always want the sunshine,
But He knows there must be rain -
We love the sound of laughter
And the merriment of cheer,
But our hearts would lose their tenderness
If we never shed a tear ...
So whenever we are troubled
And life has lost its song
It's God testing us with burdens
Just to make our spirit strong!

Helen Steiner Rice

The Home Beyond

We feel so sad when those we love
Are called to live in the home above,
But why should we grieve when they say good-bye
And go to dwell in a cloudless sky?
For they have but gone to prepare the way,
And we'll meet them again some happy day,
For God has told us that nothing can sever
A life He created to live forever.
So let God's promise soften our sorrow
And give us new strength for a brighter tomorrow.

My Birthday in Bethesda

How little we know what God has in store
As daily He blesses our lives more and more.
I've lived many years and I've learned many things,
But today I have grown new spiritual wings ...
For pain has a way of broadening our view
And bringing us closer in sympathy, too,
To those who are living in constant pain
And trying somehow to bravely sustain
The faith and endurance to keep on trying
When they almost welcome the peace of dying ...
Without this experience I would have lived and died
Without fathoming the pain of Christ crucified,
For none of us knows what pain is all about
Until our spiritual wings start to sprout.
So thank You, God, for the gift You sent
To teach me that pain's heaven-sent.

Helen Steiner Rice

Faith for Dark Days

When dark days come - and they come to us all -
We feel so helpless and lost and small.
We cannot fathom the reason why,
And it is futile for us to try
To find the answer, the reason or cause,
For the master plan is without any flaws.
And when the darkness shuts out the light,
We must lean on faith to restore our sight,
For there is nothing we need know
If we have faith that wherever we go
God will be there to help us to bear
Our disappointments, pain, and care.
For He is our shepherd, our Father, our Guide,
And you're never alone with the Lord at your side.
So may the great Physician attend you,
And may His healing completely mend you.

My Daily Prayer

God, be my resting place and my protection
In hours of trouble, defeat, and dejection.
May I never give way to self-pity and sorrow,
May I always be sure of a better tomorrow,
May I stand undaunted come what may,
Secure in the knowledge I have only to pray
And ask my Creator and Father above
To keep me serene in His grace and His love.

Helen Steiner Rice